3:16

THE NUMBERS OF HOPE

STUDY GUIDE | FIVE SESSIONS

MAX LUCADO
WITH ANDREA LUCADO

HarperChristian Resources

3:16—The Numbers of Hope Study Guide
© 2021 by Max Lucado

Requests for information should be addressed to:
HarperChristian Resources, 3900 Sparks Dr. SE, Grand Rapids, Michigan 49546

ISBN 978-0-310-12098-8 (softcover)
ISBN 978-0-310-12099-5 (ebook)

HarperChristian Resources titles may be purchased in bulk for church, business, fundraising, or ministry use. For information, please e-mail ResourceSpecialist@ChurchSource.com.

Published in association with Anvil II Management, Inc.

First Printing November 2021 / Printed in the United States of America

CONTENTS

INTRODUCTION

If you're a churchgoer, you've likely heard it a thousand times. Even if you're not the churchgoing type, you've probably seen it embroidered on a pillow or written in calligraphy on a piece of artwork. The sentence is prolific in our language and culture. But its words are more than a good saying, a favorite memory verse, or a catchy lyric. John 3:16 is the thesis of the New Testament. The climax of a theological moment. It is the Hope Diamond of the Bible.

> *For God*
> *so loved the world*
> *that he gave his one and only Son,*
> *that whoever believes in him*
> *shall not perish but have*
> *eternal life.*

There it is—a twenty-six-word parade of hope, beginning with God, ending with life, and urging us to do the same. Brief enough to write on a napkin or memorize in a moment, yet solid enough to weather two thousand years of storms and questions. If you know nothing of the Bible, start here.

If you know everything in the Bible, return here. We all need the reminder. The heart of the human problem is the heart of the human. And God's treatment is prescribed in John 3:16.

He loves.
He gave.
We believe.
We live.

Each word is a safe-deposit box of jewels. Read it again, slowly and aloud, and note the word that snatches your attention: "For God so loved the world that he gave his one and only Son, that whoever believes in him shall not perish but have eternal life."

"For God so loved the world . . ." Yes, *this* world, filled with its heartbreakers, hope-snatchers, and dream-dousers. Dictators rage. Abusers inflict. Reverends think they deserve the title. But still God *loves*. In fact, he loves the world so much he gave his:

"One and only Son . . ." The mind-bending claim of John 3:16 is that God gave not abstract ideas but a flesh-wrapped divinity. The Bible equates Jesus with God. So God, then, out of his great love for the world gave of *himself.* Why? So that:

"Whoever believes in him shall not perish." *Whoever . . .* a universal word. All are invited to receive. And *perish . . .* a sobering word. A warning of the consequences for not receiving. We'd like to dilute the term. But not Jesus. He pounds Do Not Enter signs on every square inch of Satan's gate and tells those hell-bent on entering to do so over his dead body. Even so, some souls insist—and in the end, some perish and some live. What determines the difference? Not works or talents, pedigrees, or possessions. The difference is determined by _belief_.

Bible translators in the New Hebrides islands once struggled to find an appropriate verb for _believe_. One translator, John G. Paton, accidentally came upon a solution while hunting with a tribesman. The two men bagged a large deer and carried it on a pole along a steep mountain path to Paton's home. When they reached the veranda, the men dropped the load and plopped into the porch chairs. As they did, the native exclaimed in the language of his people, "My, it is good to stretch yourself out here and rest."

Paton immediately reached for paper and pencil and recorded the phrase. As a result, his final translation of John 3:16 was worded: "For God so loved the world, that he gave his only begotten Son, that whosoever stretcheth himself out on Him should not perish, but have everlasting life."

As you go through this study and receive God's Word for you, may you do just that—stretch out on Christ and rest.

How to Use This Guide

The *3:16* video study is designed to be experienced in a group setting (such as a Bible study, Sunday school class, or small-group gathering) and also as an individual study. Each session begins with a brief opening reflection and icebreaker questions to get you and your group thinking about the topic. You will then watch a video with Max Lucado, which can be accessed via the streaming code found on the inside front cover. If you are doing the study with a group, you will then engage in some directed small-group discussion. You will close each session with a time of personal reflection and prayer as a group.

Each person in the group should have his or her own study guide, which includes video teaching notes, Bible study and group discussion questions, and between-sessions personal studies to help you reflect and apply the material to your life during the week. You are also encouraged to have a copy of the *3:16* book, as reading it alongside the curriculum will provide you with deeper insights and make the journey more meaningful. See the "recommended reading" section at the end of each session for the chapters in the book that correspond to the material you and your group are discussing.

To get the most out of your group experience, keep the following points in mind. First, the real growth in this study will happen during your small-group time. This is where you will process the video content for the week, ask questions, and learn from others as you hear what God is doing in their lives. For this reason, it is important for you to be fully committed to the group and attend each session so you can build trust and rapport with the other members. If you choose to only go through the motions, or if you refrain from participating, there is a lesser chance you will find what you're looking for during this study.

Second, remember that the goal of your small group is to serve as a place where people can share, learn about God, and build intimacy and friendship. For this reason, seek to make your group a safe place. This means being honest about your thoughts and feelings and listening carefully to everyone else's opinion. (If you are a group leader, there are additional instructions and resources in the back of the book for leading a productive discussion group.)

Third, resist the temptation to fix a problem someone might be having or to correct his or her theology, as that's not the purpose of your small-group time. Also, keep everything your group shares confidential. This will foster a rewarding sense of community in your group and create a place where people can heal, be challenged, and grow spiritually.

Following your group time, you can maximize the impact of the course with the additional between-session studies. For each session, you may wish to complete the personal study all in one sitting or spread it out over a few days (for example, working on it a half-hour a day on four different days that week). Note that if you are unable to finish (or even start) your between-sessions personal study, you should still attend the group study video session. You are still wanted and welcome at the group even if you don't have your "homework" done.

Keep in mind that the videos, discussion questions, and activities are simply meant to kick-start your imagination so you are open to what God wants you to hear and how to apply it to your life. So, as you go through this study on John 3:16, listen to what God is saying to you as you and your group explore this important verse in the Bible.

The Most Famous Conversation in the Bible

> *"A man named Nicodemus . . .*
> *came to Jesus at night."*
> John 3:1–2

Welcome

If you could go back in time, what would you change? If you got a do-over, what would you redo? Hindsight—it's 20/20. Regret—it's plentiful. With some areas, seasons, years, people, and events in our lives, we just wish we could do them again.

But in our finite bodies on this finite planet and in our finite timelines, we know going back to the past just isn't possible. So we can't blame Nicodemus for his confusion when Jesus said, "No one can see the kingdom of God unless they are born again" (John 3:3). *Be born again?* "How can someone be born when they are old?" he asked (verse 4).

In a world of no second chances, one shot, and better-get-it-right-the-first-time, it's hard to conceive of what it means to be born again. All we know is "missing the boat," "better luck next time," and "if at first you don't succeed . . ." honestly, you probably won't.

Nicodemus may not have understood it in the moment, but what he received from Jesus that night was hope. A hope to start over, be new, be clean. A chance to actually be born, again. As John explained, "For God so loved the world that he gave his one and only Son, that whoever believes in him shall not perish but have eternal life" (verse 16).

It's simple, really. But we tend to complicate it. We replace "whoever believes in him" with "whoever is good enough, smart enough, compassionate enough . . . is worthy of God's love." We take ourselves out of the equation. "My past is too questionable. No re-dos. No do-overs."

John 3:16 assures us otherwise. It brings us hope for our future and hope for today. We can be born again in this life and be born again into eternity with the God who loves us. What can be better than that? What's more, our rebirth is not up to us. If it were, there's no guarantee we would do it right the second time. It is made possible only by the power of God and through the saving grace of Jesus. When he is in charge of the do-over, the do-over is always done right.

As you take this deep dive into one of the richest verses in Scripture, may you remain open to this God whose love is so big it covers the whole world—whose love is so big it covers *you*.

SHARE

If you or any of your group members are just getting to know one another, take a few minutes to introduce yourselves. Then, to get things started, discuss one of the following questions:

- What do you associate with John 3:16? A person, a period in your life, something you've read? Why does this verse conjure that association?

— *or* —

- What immediately comes to mind when you think of John 3:16? What especially stands out to you about the verse?

READ

Invite someone to read aloud the following passage. Listen for fresh insights as you hear the verses being read and then discuss the questions that follow.

> ⁵ *"Very truly I tell you, no one can enter the kingdom of God unless they are born of water and the Spirit.* ⁶ *Flesh gives birth to flesh, but the Spirit gives birth to spirit.* ⁷ *You should not be surprised at my saying, 'You must be born again.'* ⁸ *The wind blows wherever it pleases. You hear its sound, but you cannot tell where it comes*

from or where it is going. So it is with everyone born of the Spirit."

John 3:5–8

What was one key insight that stood out to you from the Scripture? *born of flesh and spirit*

What role does the <u>Spirit play</u> in our being born again?

Talks to our heart and soul Helps us to understand more clearly.

WATCH

Play the video segment for session one (see the streaming video access provided on the inside front cover). As you watch, use the following outline to record any thoughts or concepts that stand out to you.

Nicodemus came to Jesus "<u>at night.</u>" Most of the events in the Bible—especially the important ones—happened during the day. That was the time to see and be seen, to teach and to learn, and to ask and answer. But not this discussion.

Away from everyone who would see him—Nicodemus, a ~~pharisie~~ pharisee

Nicodemus took a risk in conducting this conversation with Christ. It's a risk that all of us today should be glad he was willing to take. For out of this short discussion comes one of the most famous verses in all of the Bible.

Didn't want anyone he knew to see him talking with Jesus.

Jesus tells Nicodemus, "Very truly I tell you, no one can see the kingdom of God unless they are born again." (John 3:3). With this proclamation, Jesus carves out the Continental Divide of Scripture. The international date line of faith.

Works won't get you into heaven. "born again" — not literally. spiritually.

The Greek word that Jesus uses for again is anothen. It depicts a repeated action, but it requires the original source to repeat it. Jesus is saying the original Creator re-creates his creation. The potter reforms the clay.

from above, the one who can repeat it. Original creator, repeats it. Why?

Jesus describes the source of his testimony—that he is a witness to heavenly things and heavenly truths. He reveals that he alone has the authority to speak of heaven because he alone has come down from heaven.

— Forshadows his future

The heart of the human problem is the heart of the human—and God's prescription is found in John 3:16. *He loves. He gave. We believe. We live.*

We have all sinned !
When times get hard — remember
Jesus !

DISCUSS

Take some time with your group to discuss what you just watched and answer the following questions.

1. Before starting this study, how would you have described John 3:16 and its role in the Christian faith?

   The heart

2. What were Nicodemus' credentials in the Jewish religion and culture? Why is this important to know in the context of his conversation with Jesus?

   He is a Pharisee

3. What is the difference between the Greek words *palin* and *anothen*? Which one did Jesus use in John 3:3? What is the significance of this?

   palin — earthly
   anothen — heavenly — spiritual

4. According to John 3:3, what does it mean to be "born again"? Does this differ from how you've understood this phrase in the past? If so, how?

   to be born again spiritually

5. Read John 3:13–16. What claims are made in this passage? Which ones are easy for you to believe? Which ones are difficult for you to believe?

   No one can get into heaven except through Jesus Christ.

RESPOND

Briefly review the outline for the video teaching and any notes you took. In the space below, write down the most significant point you took away from this session.

PRAY

One of the most important things you can do together in community is to pray for each other. This is not simply a closing prayer to end your group time but a portion of time to share prayer requests, review how God has answered past prayers, and actually pray for one another. As you close your time together this week, ask God to open your hearts to receive his truth over the next several weeks. Ask him to strengthen your faith and understanding as you learn more about these life-saving words in John 3:16. Pray that the message will ring as true for you today as it did that night with Nicodemus so many years ago. Praise God that no matter what you have done in your past, we can have eternal life through the saving power of Jesus. Finally, use the space below to write down any specific prayer requests or praises for the coming week.

NAME	REQUEST / PRAISE
Victoria	bring her closer to Jesus
Quinn	open his heart and mind to Jesus

BETWEEN-SESSIONS PERSONAL STUDY

SESSION ONE

Take some time to reflect on the material you've covered this week by engaging in any or all of the following between-sessions activities. Each personal study consists of a passage of Scripture and reflection questions to help you dig deeper into this week's session. For this week, you will take a closer look at John 3:1–21 in order to understand the full context of the verse at the center of this study. The time you invest will be well spent, so let God use it to draw you closer to him. At the start of the next session, you will have a few minutes to share any insights that you learned with the group.

DAY 1: HE CAME TO JESUS AT NIGHT

This week, you were introduced to the context around John 3:16. It involved a Pharisee seeking out Jesus by cover of darkness and Christ revealing the most important of gospel truths to him. In a way, this is a strange conversation between two unlikely characters, but this brief interaction can tell us a lot about what Jesus is like and how we are invited to interact with him. Read about Nicodemus' encounter with Jesus in John 3:1–4 and answer the questions below.

> [1] *Now there was a Pharisee, a man named Nicodemus who was a member of the Jewish ruling council.* [2] *He came to Jesus at night and said, "Rabbi, we know that you are a teacher who has come from God. For no one could perform the signs you are doing if God were not with him."*
>
> [3] *Jesus replied, "Very truly I tell you, no one can see the kingdom of God unless they are born again."*
>
> [4] *"How can someone be born when they are old?" Nicodemus asked. "Surely they cannot enter a second time into their mother's womb to be born!"*

Have you ever sought Jesus out in the way Nicodemus did—with urgency (and maybe even secretly)? What were you seeking from Jesus?

guidance, understanding direction

Why do you think Nicodemus approached Jesus at night? Although the Bible doesn't tell us, what do you think he wanted from Jesus?

—He didn't want to be seen by others

— Answers and understanding

According to verse 3, how did Jesus respond to Nicodemus' praise? Why do you think Jesus responded this way?

No one can truly understand unless they are born again

Can you relate to Nicodemus' confusion in verse 4? Have you ever felt confused by something in the Bible or by something you felt God tell you? If so, explain what that experience was like.

Yes — just don't understand doesn't make sense to me.

Prayer: *Lord, thank you for the promise we have in Nicodemus, who reminds us that we can approach you at any time—day or night—and you will be available to us, ready to listen, and ready to respond with truth. May we be bold like Nicodemus and seek you for answers, guidance, assurance, and hope. Thank you for meeting us in the darkness and showing us light.*

DAY 2: HOW CAN THIS BE?

Yesterday, we left Nicodemus with a lingering question: *How can someone be born again?* Today, you will read about this phrase in John 3:5–11. We often throw around words and phrases found in our faith and in our churches that sound good, but we don't always understand what they really mean. See what you can learn about what it really means to be born again. You might be surprised by what you didn't know!

> [5] *Jesus answered, "Very truly I tell you, no one can enter the kingdom of God unless they are born of water and the Spirit.* [6] *Flesh gives birth to flesh, but the Spirit gives birth to spirit.* [7] *You should not be surprised at my saying, 'You must be born again.'* [8] *The wind blows wherever it pleases. You hear its sound, but you cannot tell where it comes from or where it is going. So it is with everyone born of the Spirit."*
>
> [9] *"How can this be?" Nicodemus asked.*
>
> [10] *"You are Israel's teacher," said Jesus, "and do you not understand these things?* [11] *Very truly I tell you, we speak of what we know, and we testify to what we have seen, but still you people do not accept our testimony."*

When is the first time you remember hearing the phrase "born again"? How has your understanding of this phrase changed between that first time and now?

What does a spiritual rebirth look like? If this is something you've experienced, describe that moment.

Who are "you people" in verse 11? Why do you think it was difficult for this group to believe in what Jesus said?

the religious leaders because He brings something new to what they were taught to believe.

Is there anything in your life that needs <u>spiritual renewal</u> or <u>rebirth</u>? A relationship, circumstance, feelings of regret, or bitterness? List those things here.

- no judgement   -patience
- loving
- understanding

Prayer: *God, thank you for the promise of new life. Even when I don't understand you, your power, or how you work, I know that as I have been born again in the Spirit, so can different areas of my life. You bring restoration to broken relationships. You bring healing to ailing bodies. You bring justice to unjust situations. Do the work of renewal in my life. Bring the wind of grace, peace, and love where I need it most. Make me new, as you do each day.*

DAY 3: LIFTED UP

In John 3:14, Jesus compared himself to the snake that Moses lifted up in the wilderness—an event described in Numbers 21:4–8. Even though the Israelites had been saved from slavery, they often complained to Moses about their journey into the desert, forgetting what God had done for them. In Numbers 21:6, God sent venomous snakes to punish the Israelites for their complaints. Then, when the Israelites cried out to be saved from the snakes, God instructed Moses to craft a bronze snake and put it on a pole. Whenever an Israelite was bitten by a snake, if he looked at the bronze snake, he would be saved from harm. With this context in mind, read John 3:12–15.

> [12] *I have spoken to you of earthly things and you do not believe; how then will you believe if I speak of heavenly things?* [13] *No one has ever gone into heaven except the one who came from heaven—the Son of Man.* [14] *Just as Moses lifted up the snake in the wilderness, so the Son of Man must be lifted up,* [15] *that everyone who believes may have eternal life in him.*

When did you first learn about salvation through Christ? How was it explained to you? How does your understanding of salvation today differ from how you originally understood it?

Considering the story from Numbers 21:4–8, how is Jesus like the bronze snake lifted up by Moses?

Those who look to him / believe in Him. Will be saved.

Nicodemus was a student of the Law and Hebrew Scriptures. He would have been familiar with this story of Moses and the bronze snake. How do you think he interpreted Jesus' comparison?

Once Jesus explained it to him, I think he would see it differently than he was taught. Sa the connection.

How does this story of Moses change or help explain how you understand salvation, our sin, and our relationship with God because of our sin?

We need Jesus! Look to him — He is lifted up by the father.

Prayer: *Father, I confess salvation can be a hard concept for me to understand and believe. Some days, I feel overwhelmed by my sin and am so grateful for my salvation. Other days, I feel like I can do this on my own because I'm a good person and don't need salvation. And many days, I fall somewhere in between.*

Help me understand the saving nature of Jesus. I have learned about it a dozen times, but let this lesson take up residence in my heart. May I feel it and believe it and know that it is true on days that I let my sin get the best of me and on days when my sin is believing that I have none.

DAY 4: COME INTO THE LIGHT

In John 3:16–21, the basis of the Christian faith is explained. Who God is, who Jesus is, and what that means for our sin is laid out in a clear picture for Nicodemus and for us. While John 3:16 is one of the first verses we learn when we become a Christian, we can still confuse the roles of the Father, the Son, and our own in the context of our salvation and eternity. Read the passage and be on the lookout for new insights and revelations.

[16] For God so loved the world that he gave his one and only Son, that whoever believes in him shall not perish but have eternal life. [17] For God did not send his Son into the world to condemn the world, but to save the world through him. [18] Whoever believes in him is not condemned, but whoever does not believe stands condemned already because they have not believed in the name of God's one and only Son. [19] This is the verdict: Light has come into the world, but people loved darkness instead of light because their deeds were evil. [20] Everyone who does evil hates the light, and will not come into the light for fear that their deeds will be exposed. [21] But whoever lives by the truth comes into the light, so that it may be seen plainly that what they have done has been done in the sight of God.

How do you feel about your salvation today? Do you believe completely that Jesus has saved you? Are you unsure due to your past or current sin? Are you unsure because you're not sure what you believe theologically about salvation and how it works? Explain your response.

> Yes, I believe. Sometimes I doubt, but that is Satan trying to deceive me.

According to this passage, why did God send his Son into the world and how are we saved by him?

> He sent his son into the world to save us. He was and is the pure lamb that was slain for our sins.

How did Jesus bring light to the world?

> Through him being on this earth, his love, compassion, miracles, truth.

What did you learn about God in this passage? What did you learn about Jesus? What did you learn about your own sin or darkness?

God gave his Son, Jesus to us to save us from our sin so we can be with Him in heaven and eternity.

Prayer: *Dear God, your verdict is light. You have tried us. You have seen our sin and still, in your love, you bring us into the light of Christ. Thank you for this truth. Thank you that my sin does not have to stay in darkness and that when it is brought into the light, it is done away with for good. Help me believe this. Free me from the yoke of my own sin and regret and remind me of yours—the one that is easy and light.*

FOR NEXT WEEK

Use the space below to write any key points or questions you want to bring to the next group meeting. In preparation for next week, read chapters 3–4 in *3:16*.

HOPE FOR THE HARD HEART

"For God so loved the world . . ."
John 3:16

WELCOME

You've heard it said that "it is better to give than to receive." When it comes to humans and love, the saying could be similar: "It is easier to give love than to receive it." You love your children unconditionally. You are delighted by them. But the idea of being delighted in or being loved despite your faults and shortcomings . . . well, that can make you squirm.

Yet the Bible says this is exactly how God loves you! Not because you deserve his love, but simply because he wants to love you. He chose to love you—and continues to do so—every day. Often, the only thing standing in the way between you and God's love is you.

In today's session, we will discuss the power of *agape* love. This is a divine love—the essence of God represented in the person of Jesus Christ. But because it is divine, it can be difficult for us to understand. And in our lack of understanding, we turn to other things to fill us with the love that we desperately crave: *idols*. Just as the Israelites who worshiped the golden calf in the wilderness, we worship celebrities and our social media followings and money and whatever else brings us temporary pleasure. It's easier and less vulnerable to seek love in these places rather than confess our own inadequacy and accept the unconditional love of God.

But it is not money, followers, and fame that will save us. It is only *agape*—a love that can pull us out of the shame that causes our very rejection of that love. *Agape* answers *yes* when we ask, "Can God love me even though I hurt that other person with my words?" It says *yes* when we wonder, "Can God love me even though I've been unemployed for over a year?" It responds yes when we fear, "Can God love me even though I am divorced, scarred, a victim, a failure . . . ?" *Yes, yes, yes.* "For God so loved [*agape*] the world."

Allowing God to love us can be more difficult than hardening our hearts toward that love. But if we harden our hearts, we miss the promise of John 3:16—a promise that isn't earned or deserved but freely given. So, instead, let's soften our hearts and receive this gift!

SHARE

If you or any of your group members are just getting to know one another, take a few minutes to introduce yourselves and then share any insights you have from last week's personal study. Then, to get things started, discuss one of the following questions:

- What modern convenience do you complain about the most often? Something you are "hard-hearted" or "stiff-necked" toward?

— *or* —

- Do you agree with the statement, "It is easier to give love than to receive it"? Why or why not?

READ

Invite someone to read aloud the following passage. Listen for fresh insights as you hear the verses being read and then discuss the questions that follow.

> [6] *For when we were still without strength, in due time Christ died for the ungodly.* [7] *For scarcely for a righteous man will one die; yet perhaps for a good man someone would even dare to die.* [8] *But God demonstrates his own love toward us, in that while we were still sinners, Christ died for us.* [9] *Much more then, having now been justified by his blood, we shall be saved from wrath through him.*
>
> Romans 5:6–9 (NKJV)

What was one key insight that stood out to you from the Scripture? *Christ died for sinners, not just the righteous — but for ALL!*

How does this passage represent *agape* love?

divine love — decision love

WATCH

Play the video segment for session two (see the streaming video access provided on the inside front cover). As you watch, use the following outline to record any thoughts or concepts that stand out to you.

All of us have been guilty of having a <u>hard heart</u>. Consider all the wonders of our modern world. When was the last time you stepped back from your daily routine to recognize that your daily routine is saturated in marvels?

God went over and above to earn the Israelites' trust. The former slaves witnessed a millennium of miracles in a matter of days. But did they appreciate what they had received? *Maybe at first, but then No! How fast they forget!*

Thankfully, there is a <u>cure for our hardness of heart.</u> "For God so loved the world that he gave his one and only Son, that whoever believes in him shall not perish but have <u>eternal life</u>" (John 3:16).

Agape is a divine love. A perfect love. Less an affection and more a decision. Less a feeling and more an action. Agape love is a reflection of God's own nature.

loved — world

Don't be blind & resist God's love

The object of God's love is the _world_. The Greek term that John uses is _kosmos_, and he employs it here to define the scope of this love that God offers. This love is _universal_. It is extended to all humanity.

includes all — no restrictions

God doesn't remove his love if we fall into old habits, temptations, and fears. No, he demonstrates his love by continually reaching out to us—extending his invitation to get us back on the right path when we falter.

Are you living with a hard heart? Take it to the father. Amen

DISCUSS

Take some time with your group to discuss what you just watched and answer the following questions.

1. Read Exodus 32:1–7. Why did the Israelites ask Aaron to make a god for them? How does this story often mimic our own reactions toward God's love?

   Because they were impatient and couldn't wait for Moses to return to lead them.

2. Read Ephesians 4:17–19. How can hardheartedness toward God's love lead to living the life described in these verses?

We are selfish by nature. Thinking only of ourselves and not others or God.

3. What are some idols that people use today to fill their desire for unconditional love?

money, things, people

4. The Hebrew word for God's love (*hasaq*) describes a tethered and binding connection. The Greek word for God's love (*agape*) describes less a feeling and more an action. How do these two definitions help you understand the nature of God and his love?

love is an action

5. What are some things that tend to keep you from receiving God's *agape* love?

guilt, unworthiness

RESPOND

Briefly review the outline for the video teaching and any notes you took. In the space below, write down the most significant point you took away from this session.

PRAY

As you close your time together this week, take a few moments to reflect on any lies you might believe about yourself that have made you hard-hearted toward God's love. Try to think about the origin of these lies. Where did they come from? (Critical words from a family member? Misunderstood or misquoted Scripture?) If you feel comfortable, share one of these lies, and then pray for one another by replacing this lie with truth about God's love. Use the space below to write down any specific prayer requests or praises for the coming week.

NAME	REQUEST / PRAISE

BETWEEN-SESSIONS PERSONAL STUDY

SESSION TWO

Reflect on the material you've covered this week by engaging in any or all of the following between-sessions activities. Each personal study consists of a passage of Scripture and reflection questions to help you dig deeper into this week's session. The time you invest will be well spent, so let God use it to draw you closer to him. At your next meeting, share any key points or insights that stood out to you as you spent this time with the Lord.

DAY 1: OUR GOLDEN CALVES

In this week's group session, you read about the golden calf that Aaron crafted to please the Israelites' desire for an idol to worship while Moses was away. God's wrath was strong against the Israelites when they did this. The worship of idols was forbidden in the Ten Commandments, which Moses was about to present to the people a few verses later. Read in Exodus 32:7–10 what God had to say about the Israelites' rebellion and then answer the questions below.

⁷ And the LORD said to Moses, "Go, get down! For your people whom you brought out of the land of Egypt have corrupted themselves. ⁸ They have turned aside quickly out of the way which I commanded them. They have made themselves a molded calf, and worshiped it and sacrificed to it, and said, 'This is your god, O Israel, that brought you out of the land of Egypt!'" ⁹ And the LORD said to Moses, "I have seen this people, and indeed it is a stiff-necked people! ¹⁰ Now therefore, let Me alone, that My wrath may burn hot against them and I may consume them. And I will make of you a great nation" (NKJV).

How would you define *idols* in a biblical context?

Something that you worship instead of God.

What words or phrases did God use to describe the Israelites, what they had done, and how he felt about their actions?

- Corrupted themselves
- stiff-necked people
- angry — will consume them

Why do you think God was so angry at the Israelites?

Because he just saved them out of Egypt, and a short time later, they forget about the God who saved them

Consider some of the idols that you might be holding—anything you "worship" other than God. How does this passage explain the way that God feels about those idols in your life?

material things

Prayer: *Father, I confess my idols to you. My idols of money, recognition, power, beauty, and pleasure. I confess I have put these desires above my desire for you. Forgive me for letting these idols get in the way of your love for me. Forgive me for turning to them when what I really want and need is to be fully accepted for who I am. I know you love me in this way. Help me accept your love and turn from my idolatry. I declare you today as my only God, my only hope, and my only way.*

DAY 2: THE STUBBORN HEART

Jesus is the embodiment of God's love. He provided a flesh-and-blood example of what it means to be loved by God and how God feels about us. Yet in the New Testament, we read about a group who are often depicted as being resistant to this embodiment. The Pharisees were skeptical of Jesus and how he went against the laws of the Torah—even though he did so in the name of love. Read the following story in Mark 3:1–6 about Jesus' healing a man on the Sabbath and then answer the questions below.

¹ Another time Jesus went into the synagogue, and a man with a shriveled hand was there. ² Some of them were looking for a reason to accuse Jesus, so they watched him closely to see if he would heal him on the Sabbath. ³ Jesus said to the man with the shriveled hand, "Stand up in front of everyone."

⁴ Then Jesus asked them, "Which is lawful on the Sabbath: to do good or to do evil, to save life or to kill?" But they remained silent.

⁵ He looked around at them in anger and, deeply distressed at their stubborn hearts, said to the man, "Stretch out your hand." He stretched it out, and his hand was completely restored. ⁶ Then the Pharisees went out and began to plot with the Herodians how they might kill Jesus.

While Jesus is the perfect example of God's love, even in Christianity we can choose legalism, rules, and orthodoxy over loving our neighbor. Have you ever chosen religious legalism at the expense of loving someone else? If so, describe the experience and how you and the other person were affected.

I'm sure I have, but I can't remember.

Perhaps you've experienced this in the opposite way. You've been ignored, left out, or outcast in the name of religion. If so, what was that experience like for you?

According to verse 5, how did Jesus feel about the Pharisees' stubborn hearts? Why do you think he felt so strongly about this?

He was angry and deeply distressed at their stubborn hearts. It was wrong.

Why do you think the Pharisees' hearts were so hard toward Jesus even after seeing Jesus heal the man's hand?

Because they were so legalistic about the law, they miss the love.

Are there any places in your heart that are hard toward Jesus, his love, or his healing power? If so, what caused your heart to harden?

Don't understand why evil or evil people get away with their evil plans.

Prayer: *Lord, soften my heart toward you today. I confess I have chosen legalism over love. I have chosen rules and boundaries rather than reaching out to my neighbor who is different from me. I have chosen safety and security over helping others in my community. Take the Pharisee out of my heart. Replace it with your radical love for the outcast, the sick, the brokenhearted, and the poor. If you have loved me—the mess that I am—I can love others. Show me who I can love today.*

DAY 3: AGAPE

The Greek word translated as "love" in John 3:16 is *agape*. *Agape* is divine love. As you heard in this week's teaching it is a "perfect love . . . less an affection and more a decision . . . less a feeling and more an action. *Agape* love is a reflection of God's own nature." This understanding is crucial to understanding the promise of John 3:16. The following verses use *agape* in the original Greek translation. Read each passage and answer the questions below.

Matthew 22:37–40: *³⁷ Jesus replied: "'Love the Lord your God with all your heart and with all your soul and with all your mind.' ³⁸ This is the first and greatest commandment. ³⁹ And the second is like it: 'Love your neighbor as yourself.' ⁴⁰ All the Law and the Prophets hang on these two commandments."*

John 3:16: *For God so loved the world that he gave his one and only Son, that whoever believes in him shall not perish but have eternal life.*

Ephesians 2:4–5: *⁴ But because of his great love for us, God, who is rich in mercy, ⁵ made us alive with Christ even when we were dead in transgressions—it is by grace you have been saved.*

1 John 3:16–18: *¹⁶ This is how we know what love is: Jesus Christ laid down his life for us. And we ought to lay down our lives for our brothers and sisters. ¹⁷ If anyone has material possessions and sees a brother or sister in need but has no pity on them, how can the love of God be in that person? ¹⁸ Dear children, let us not love with words or speech but with actions and in truth.*

What is the best example of love that you have witnessed? Why is this the best example to you?

What do these verses reveal about how and why God loves you?

– died for me, even a sinner.
– has mercy and forgiveness

What do these verses reveal about how you are instructed to love others with *agape* love?

Love your neighbor as yourself.

What are some ways that you love God and love others well? What are some ways you could love God and love others better?

Prayer: *God, thank you for loving me with your agape love. Thank you for choosing to love me every day even though I sin and fall short every day. Teach me more about your love through your Son, Jesus. Help me love as he loves. Help me see others as he sees them. Deepen my understanding of you and your boundless, endless, sacrificial love. May your love be my motivation and power to love others in the same way.*

DAY 4: THE WHOLE WORLD

God loves you with his *agape* love, but you must choose to receive it. Your past, your sin, and your shortcomings will try to convince you that you are not worthy of love from other people and not worthy of love from a perfect God. But that is the voice of the enemy, who would love for you to believe you aren't enough. The voice of Christ says you are always enough in him. Read the following verses about God's love for you and then answer the questions below.

Romans 8:38–39: *38 For I am convinced that neither death nor life, neither angels nor demons, neither the present nor the future, nor any powers, 39 neither height nor depth, nor anything else in all creation, will be able to separate us from the love of God that is in Christ Jesus our Lord.*

Ephesians 3:17–19: *17 And I pray that you, being rooted and established in love, 18 may have power, together with all the Lord's holy people, to grasp how wide and long and high and deep is the love of Christ, 19 and to know this love that surpasses knowledge—that you may be filled to the measure of all the fullness of God.*

1 John 4:16–18: *16 God is love. Whoever lives in love lives in God, and God in them. 17 This is how love is made complete among us so that we will have confidence on the day of judgment: In this world we are like Jesus. 18 There is no fear in love. But perfect love drives out fear, because fear has to do with punishment.*

What lie are you believing today (or in the past) that has made you think you are unworthy of God's love?

not good enough

How do Romans 8:38–39 and Ephesians 3:17–19 describe God's love?

Nothing can separate us from the love of God. God's love is never ending.

What do you think John meant when he wrote, "There is no fear in love" (1 John 4:18)?

God is not fear, His love is not fear. There is no fear in God.

How would you feel about yourself, others, and God if you believed without a doubt that God loved you fully and unconditionally in the way these verses describe? What would change?

I would live more freely.

Prayer: *Dear God, although you have offered me your full, unconditional, and boundless love, I admit it is hard for me to accept. I don't deserve it. You know I don't deserve it, even on my best days. Help me get over myself. Help me look past my past. Help me receive your love—your love that heals the shame I so often feel. Help me move from the place of trying to earn love to the place of just being loved. I know you have already given me this good and perfect gift. May I accept it as my own.*

FOR NEXT WEEK

Use the space below to write any key points or questions you want to bring to the next group meeting. In preparation for next week, read chapters 5–6 from *3:16.*

THE HEART HE OFFERS

"He gave his one and only Son . . ."
John 3:16

WELCOME

What is your "one and only"? An item of which you only own one? Maybe it is your one and only car. Your one and only computer. Your one and only diamond ring. Your one and only cell phone. Your one and only treasured keepsake from a parent or friend. Your one and only _____. You fill in the blank.

How much more valuable are these one-and-onlys as compared to your one-in-severals? Shoes, socks, pens—these are all easily replaced. But your one-and-only items? Those you treasure and protect. You keep them close to you and in a safe place. If you lose them, you panic. If they are stolen, you are distraught, because you don't have a backup. You only have one.

In John 3:16, we read that Jesus is God's "one and only Son." The Bible doesn't say that Jesus is just one of many sons of God, or that he provides one of many ways to the

Father, or that speaks one of many truths. He is God's *only* begotten Son, the *only* way to the Father, and the *only* truth (see John 14:6–7). This makes Jesus invaluable not only to God but also to us.

There are some people who say that Jesus was just a good teacher, a good leader, and a good person all around. He said and did some wonderful things, many of which were written down and recorded for history . . . and that's the end of the story. But if you truly believe the words of John 3:16—that Jesus was God's one and only Son—then it changes everything. You believe Jesus was not only a good guy but that he was *the* guy. The Son. The way. The truth. The life. The one and only.

It's a simple phrase. Only a few words in the verse that we are studying that at first glance seem insignificant to the ones around it. But they are crucial words that reveal a crucial truth. If we want to be saved, if we want to be healed, and if we want to know the way to eternal life, then we must believe in the *one and only*—and that one and only is Jesus.

SHARE

Begin your time by inviting those in the group to share any insights they had from last week's personal study. Then, to get things started, discuss one of the following questions:

- What is your most valuable one-and-only possession? Why is it so valuable to you? *wedding ring*

— or —

- Why is it important to recognize that Jesus was God's one and only Son? *Because He is the only way to heaven.*

READ

Invite someone to read aloud the following passage. Listen for fresh insights as you hear the verses being read and then discuss the questions that follow.

> *¹⁰ As it is written:*
>
> > *"There is no one righteous,*
> > *not even one;*
> > *¹¹ there is no one who understands;*
> > *there is no one who seeks God.*
> > *¹² All have turned away,*
> > *they have together become worthless;*
> > *there is no one who does good,*
> > *not even one."*
>
> Romans 3:10–12

What was one key insight that stood out to you from the Scripture?

No one is righteous or good.

Do you feel any resistance to this claim: "there is no one who does good, not even one"? Why or why not?

we are sinful people

WATCH

Play the video segment for session three (see the streaming video access provided on the inside front cover). As you watch, use the following outline to record any thoughts or concepts that stand out to you.

NOTES

When there's something wrong with the core of who you are, it's a big problem. It is a condition that cannot be ignored. So you need a spiritual checkup—and not from the cardiologist down the road but from the God of heaven.

the heart is deceitful

We are heart sick and heart sunk, with no hope of recovery on our own. We need help. But how do we find that help? What kind of spiritual surgeon is on call?

John 3:16

Jesus

— heart sick and heart sunk

" one and only "

Jesus alone is the <u>monogenetic</u> Son of God. He alone has God's genes or genetic makeup. Every quality we attribute to God, we can attribute to Jesus.

Anyone who has Seen me, has $seen the father.

How often have we seen Jesus touch our lives? How often have we received more than we could ever ask or imagine? Yet how often do we fail to submit to him and acknowledge his lordship over our lives?

The issue is one of authority
Luke 7:7-8

The Roman officer saluted Christ as the supreme commander. And Jesus didn't correct him! Christ claims ultimate clout. Unshared supremacy.

faith in Christ

<u>Christ gave himself for you</u>. Specifically, he exchanged hearts *with* you. Mind you, this is no transplant but a swap. *Christ for us*

1 Cor 15:3
Gal 1:4
3:13
John 10:11

Luke 22:19
22:20

DISCUSS

Take some time with your group to discuss what you just watched and answer the following questions.

1. After watching today's lesson, how would you define the relationship between God and Jesus? Is this different from your previous understanding? If so, how?

    They are the same

2. Read John 14:6–10. Why do you think the disciples were confused about Jesus' identity even after spending three years in ministry with him?

    They didn't understand Jesus was the same as God.

3. What doubts or questions do you have about Jesus, who he is, and who he was while on earth?

    His timing is not my timing.

4. What does the word *authority* bring to your mind? How does it make you feel?

    Someone in charge

5. Read Luke 7:1–10. How is Jesus' authority explained and displayed in this story? How does this help you understand Christ as an authority in your own life?

What Christ says will be done.

RESPOND

Briefly review the outline for the video teaching and any notes you took. In the space below, write down the most significant point you took away from this session.

Jesus took our sin upon himself.

PRAY

As you close your time together this week, ask God to reveal more of his character to you. Pray that he will show you who he really is and help you to better understand his ways, his power, and his truth. Ask him to be with you in your doubts—knowing that he welcomes them because they invite you to dig deeper into his truth and discover more about your nature and the Father's. Pray that he will bring you comfort as you sit with your doubts and resist the temptation to solve them, ignore them, or hide them. Use the space below to write down any specific prayer requests or praises for the coming week.

Name	Request / Praise

BETWEEN-SESSIONS PERSONAL STUDY

SESSION THREE

Reflect on the material you've covered this week by engaging in any or all of the following between-sessions activities. Each personal study consists of a passage of Scripture and reflection questions to help you dig deeper into this week's session. The time you invest will be well spent, so let God use it to draw you closer to him. At your next meeting, share any key points or insights that stood out to you as you spent this time with the Lord.

DAY 1: THE WAY

Jesus told his disciples, "I am the way and the truth and the life" (John 14:6). This is true for our salvation and eternity as well as our lives today. We all want to know the way forward, to know what is true, and how to live our lives in a full and meaningful way. So, for this week's personal study, we'll be digging into this verse, starting with what it means for Jesus to be "the way." When we don't know the way forward, when are stuck on the backward path of regret, when we don't know what to do next, how might Jesus show us the way? Read the following passages and then answer the questions below.

John 15:4–5: *⁴ Remain in me, as I also remain in you. No branch can bear fruit by itself; it must remain in the vine. Neither can you bear fruit unless you remain in me.*

⁵ "I am the vine; you are the branches. If you remain in me and I in you, you will bear much fruit; apart from me you can do nothing."

Hebrews 4:14–16: *¹⁴ Therefore, since we have a great high priest who has ascended into heaven, Jesus the Son of God, let us hold firmly to the faith we profess. ¹⁵ For we do not have a high priest who is unable to empathize with our weaknesses, but we have one who has been tempted in every way, just as we are—yet he did not sin. ¹⁶ Let us then approach God's throne of grace with confidence, so that we may receive mercy and find grace to help us in our time of need.*

2 Corinthians 5:17–18: *¹⁷ Therefore, if anyone is in Christ, the new creation has come: The old has gone, the new is here! ¹⁸ All this is from God, who reconciled us to himself through Christ and gave us the ministry of reconciliation.*

How are you struggling to find your way right now? Are you in the midst of a big decision and you're not sure what to do? Do you feel trapped by past regret and can't seem to find your way forward? Describe what difficulty you are having with finding your way in your life and community.

making a commitment
volunteer at church

What do these verses tell you about how Jesus can help you find your way?

- remain in Him, you will bear
fruit.
- He knows our weakness

What do these verses tell you about who you are because of Jesus and what he did?

We are a new Creation
the old is gone!

Considering these passages, how could Jesus help guide you in a new way today?

Ask Him!

Prayer: *Lord, you are my one and only way. You are my way to eternity, and you are my way today—right here, right now. Show me where you want me to go. Let me know if I am on the wrong the path. I know that you are my great high priest. Therefore, you intercede on my behalf with the Father. Intercede on my behalf today. Put me on the path that glorifies you by showing others grace, mercy, and love. Thank you that I can always be confident in my next step because you are guiding me there.*

DAY 2: THE TRUTH

Jesus said he is the *truth*. In today's world of social media, countless news outlets, memes, and information all claiming to convey a truth, it can be hard to sift through and know what really is true. Jesus is the perfect example of someone who brought both truth and grace to the world. His truth was life-giving, caring, and loving. Read the following passages from the Gospel about Jesus and truth and then answer the questions below.

> **John 1:14:** *The Word became flesh and made his dwelling among us. We have seen his glory, the glory of the one and only Son, who came from the Father, full of grace and truth.*

> **John 4:23–24:** *23 Yet a time is coming and has now come when the true worshipers will worship the Father in the Spirit and in truth, for they are the kind of worshipers the Father seeks. 24 God is spirit, and his worshipers must worship in the Spirit and in truth.*

John 8:31–32: *31 To the Jews who had believed him, Jesus said, "If you hold to my teaching, you are really my disciples. 32 Then you will know the truth, and the truth will set you free."*

Where do you typically go for the truth? A news outlet, social media, the Bible, a wise friend? Why is this your go-to source?

Bible and friends
It is truth

How was Jesus full of both grace and truth (see John 1:14)?

He was/is perfect.

What does it mean to worship in spirit and in truth?

With your whole heart,
soul and mind, body.

If the litmus test for truth is that it will set you free (John 8:32), what truths can you depend on in your life today?

Jesus set me free
He is my savior & redeemer.

Prayer: *Father, you sent us your Son to show us truth and grace. Point me to your truth today. There is so much noise around me. So much anger, finger pointing, confusion, and differing information. I often don't know how to sort through it all on my own. But even when I'm not sure what the truth is out there, I can be certain of what is in here, in me: Jesus. He will show me the way. He will guide me to truth and that truth will not feel like bondage or a burden. That truth will set me free. Thank you for the guide you have given me in Jesus, my true north.*

DAY 3: THE LIFE

Jesus said that he is the _life_. Many of us have dreams of what kind of life we want to live. And many of us have experienced life not turning out the way we thought it would. How can we live a good and full life? How do we do this when there is so much disappointment, difficulty, death, and hardship around us? Jesus also said, "I have come that they may have life, and have it to the full" (John 10:10). What did Jesus mean by this? That we would go on big adventures, live life to the fullest, and seize the day? Perhaps, but other verses in Scripture illuminate the type of life Jesus invites you to enter. Read those passages and then answer the questions that follow.

John 4:13–15: *13 Jesus answered, "Everyone who drinks this water will be thirsty again, 14 but whoever drinks the water I give them will never thirst. Indeed, the water I give them will become in them a spring of water welling up to eternal life."*

15 The woman said to him, "Sir, give me this water so that I won't get thirsty and have to keep coming here to draw water."

John 6:32–35: *32 Jesus said to them, "Very truly I tell you, it is not Moses who has given you the bread from heaven, but it is my Father who gives you the true bread from heaven. 33 For the bread of God is the bread that comes down from heaven and gives life to the world."*

34 "Sir," they said, "always give us this bread."

35 Then Jesus declared, "I am the bread of life. Whoever comes to me will never go hungry, and whoever believes in me will never be thirsty."

Matthew 11:28–30: *28 "Come to me, all you who are weary and burdened, and I will give you rest. 29 Take my yoke upon you and learn from me, for I am gentle and humble in heart, and you will find rest for your souls. 30 For my yoke is easy and my burden is light."*

What activities or people are life-giving for you? Why?

Praising, worshipping
Walking

How is Jesus our bread of life and our living water? Have you experienced him in this way? If so, how?

He feeds us everyday, through his words.

What is Jesus' invitation for us in Matthew 11:28–30? What would it look like for you to receive this invitation?

Give Jesus your troubles, problems, concerns and He will carry them.

According to these verses, what do you think Jesus' vision is for us to "have life and have it to the full" (John 10:10)?

We can have our fullest life by following, listening and obeying Jesus.

Prayer: *Father, thank you for sending Jesus into this world—the one who quenches our spiritual thirst and provides springs of eternal life. Thank you for the promise that Jesus is the bread of life who satisfies all of our spiritual hunger for your truth. Thank you for the offer that when we are weary and burdened, we can come to you for rest. Today, I choose to rest in your promises and accept the life-giving water and bread that Jesus offers to me.*

DAY 4: OUR HELP AND HEALING

Jesus is the one and only way to truth and life. He is also our one and only hope for healing. As you saw in this week's teaching, the nature of the spiritual operation that needs to be performed in order to heal us hinges on the Greek word *hyper*, which means "in place of" or "on behalf of." Jesus has offered us spiritual healing by taking on the punishment for our sin. We are no longer slaves to our sin because of this healing. This is good news, but we must believe it or else we will continue to live by hate, fear, and anger. Review the following passages that translate the Greek word *hyper* as "for" and answer the questions below.

Luke 22:19–20: *19 And he took bread, gave thanks and broke it, and gave it to them, saying, "This is my body given for you; do this in remembrance of me."*

20 In the same way, after the supper he took the cup, saying, "This cup is the new covenant in my blood, which is poured out for you."

1 Corinthians 15:3–4: *3 For what I received I passed on to you as of first importance: that Christ died for our sins according to the Scriptures, 4 that he was buried, that he was raised on the third day according to the Scriptures.*

Galatians 3:13–14: *13 Christ redeemed us from the curse of the law by becoming a curse for us, for it is written: "Cursed is everyone who is hung on a pole." 14 He redeemed us in order that the blessing given to Abraham might come to the Gentiles* *through Christ Jesus, so that by faith we might receive the promise of the Spirit.*

What are some spiritual ailments in your life in which you need Jesus to bring healing? A sin pattern, guilt for the past, perpetual anger—what is it that is making your heart sick?

impatience, ~~anger~~
anger, but why?
Selfishness

According to these verses, what did Jesus do on your behalf?

forgive them all

According to Galatians 3:14, why did he do this?

So that we may receive
the blessing promised to
Abraham through faith
in Christ Jesus.

Do you believe Jesus' sacrifice can heal the spiritual ailment you suffer from today? Why or why not?

Yes!

He says he would. I just need to believe.

Prayer: *Dear God, you sent your Son to die on my behalf. Because of Jesus, I am no longer cursed by my sin. I am no longer crushed by the weight of a law that I could not live up to. I am free. Yet I still feel sick. I still suffer from the spiritual ailments of anger, hatred, fear, or despair. I need help. I need healing. Jesus, I invite you to be my healer. I believe in your healing power. Place your hand over my anger, hatred, fear, and despair. Replace my ailments with hope, love, peace, and mercy. I am no longer a slave to my sin because you poured out your life for me. Thank you for your sacrifice. Thank you for my life.*

FOR NEXT WEEK

Use the space below to write any key points or questions you want to bring to the next group meeting. In preparation for next week, read chapters 7–9 in *3:16*.

HEAVEN'S "WHOEVER" POLICY

"Whoever believes in him . . ."
John 3:16

WELCOME

In this life, to get where you want to go, you typically have to be *somebody*—a person with desirable skills, talents, abilities, degrees, and intelligence. Very little in life is offered to just *whoever*. You have to show the world that you've earned it!

Perhaps this is why the policy of heaven laid out in John 3:16 seems too good to be true: "Whoever believes in him shall not perish." *Whoever? Really?* It sounds like all the other too-good-to-be-true promises out there. "No money down. No credit required. No questions asked!" And we all know that when something *seems* too good to be true . . . it *is* too good to be true. But not so with the offer that Christ makes—the offer of who gets to receive his eternal life.

It is an uncomplicated and freeing promise. Even so, it is a truth we often find hard to believe. After all, as residents of this world, we are influenced by the attitudes of this world. As a result, we tend to fall in line with the world's thinking that we somehow need to *earn* the good things we receive in life. So, we work harder. We take on more than we can handle. We set an unattainable standard of perfection. All in an effort to be that "somebody" we desire to be.

All the while, God is saying, "Whoever believes . . . shall not perish." He takes us as we are—in the current state that he finds us—and then begins to make us born-again creations in him. The promise of John 3:16 is we can receive *life* if we put our faith in Christ. And this not just a promise for eternity. It is also a promise for *today*. We *can* experience God's abundant life in our everyday lives . . . right here on this earth.

The Bible states, "You are a chosen people, a royal priesthood, a holy nation, God's special possession" (1 Peter 2:9). As you explore heaven's "whoever" policy in this session, think about what it would look like if you believed this truth about yourself and saw yourself this way. Think about what would change if you believed what God's Word says is true— and how it would change your behaviors, priorities, and the way you felt about yourself, others, and God.

SHARE

Begin your time by inviting those in the group to share any insights they had from last week's personal study. Then, to get things started, discuss one of the following questions:

- Have you ever experienced a truly "whoever" culture—a place where anyone was welcome at any time? If so, what was it like to be a part of that community?

— *or* —

- What type of exclusivity have you experienced in life— places where only certain people belonged? What was that like for you, whether you were included or not?

READ

Invite someone to read aloud the following passage. Listen for fresh insights as you hear the verses being read and then discuss the questions that follow.

> [25] *"The works I do in my Father's name testify about me,* [26] *but you do not believe because you are not my sheep.* [27] *My sheep listen to my voice; I know them, and they follow me.* [28] *I give them eternal life, and they shall never perish; no one will snatch them out of my hand.* [29] *My Father, who has given them to me, is greater than all; no one can snatch them out of my Father's hand.* [30] *I and the Father are one."*
>
> John 10:25–30

What key insight from the Scripture stood out to you?

- my sheep listen to my
→ voice.
- no one can snatch them out
of my hand

What is the significance of the sheep and shepherd metaphor in this passage? *we are the sheep and Christ is the shepard*

WATCH

Play the video segment for session four (see the streaming video access provided on the inside front cover). As you watch, use the following outline to record any thoughts or concepts that stand out to you.

NOTES

All of us have sinned, so all of us are faced with the imminent threat of spending eternity in hell. This is why the promise of John 3:16 is so important. It is the only way for us to avoid the eternal reality of "perish."

make a declaration in Christ

God's gospel has a "whoever" policy, and it also boasts a "however" clause. God takes us *however he finds us.* No need to clean up or climb up—just look up.

whoever — all people
however — just as we are

God's gospel also comes with "whenever" and "wherever" benefits. *Whenever* we hear God's voice, he welcomes our response. *Wherever* we go in this life, we are never too far to receive his grace.

How do we receive it?
just / to believe

Our part in God's whoever policy is to believe in what Jesus has done on the cross. The idea doesn't always sit well with us. We gravitate to other verbs. Is it really as simple as allowing our Father to lead us home? *just believe*

Just as poison-corrupted Israelites found healing by looking up at the pole, so sinners will find healing by looking up to Christ. Everyone. Whoever believes. *healing to those who believed in Christ. God*

Jesus cleared a one-of-a-kind passageway uncluttered by human effort. He came not for the strong, but for the weak—not for the righteous, but for the sinner. We enter his way upon confession of our need, not on completion of our deeds.

⋆ Jesus is the only one who saves!

DISCUSS

Take some time with your group to discuss what you just watched and answer the following questions.

1. The "whoever" policy of heaven implies several other "___ ever" words. What are they? Which one resonates with you and your faith the most? Why?

All is accepted to who believe.

2. John 3:16 says, "whoever believes in him will not perish." How would you define _belief_? What does it mean, or look like, to believe in the way this passage suggests?

   trust, obey

3. It is often hard to accept that belief is all we need to be saved by God when we are accustomed to working for what we get. What is one "work"—an achievement, talent, or skill—you value about yourself? How does today's passage change your perception of this work?

4. Read Numbers 21:4–9. How does the bronze snake on the pole symbolize Jesus?

   Look up to Him and you will be healed and saved.

5. Considering the culture and times in which we live, what do you think about the idea emphasized in this session that salvation only comes through Christ? Do you push back on this idea? Do you fully accept it? Are you unsure? Explain your response.

   There are times of unbelief. Daily I must belief.

HEAVEN'S "WHOEVER" POLICY

RESPOND

Briefly review the outline for the video teaching and any notes you took. In the space below, write down the most significant point you took away from this session.

PRAY

As you close your time together this week, thank God for extending his "whoever" policy to you. Pray that you will never lose the wonder of God's grace, or dismiss its impact on your life, or overlook it in your interactions with others. Also ask God to show you ways this week that you can reach out to those who are lost and in need of heaven's whoever policy. Pray that he will use you to guide these lost sheep into his "flock." Use the space below to write down any specific prayer requests or praises for the coming week.

NAME	REQUEST / PRAISE

BETWEEN-SESSIONS
PERSONAL STUDY

SESSION FOUR

Reflect on the material you've covered this week by engaging in any or all of the following between-sessions activities. Each personal study consists of a passage of Scripture and reflection questions to help you dig deeper into this week's session. The time you invest will be well spent, so let God use it to draw you closer to him. At your next meeting, share any key points or insights that stood out to you as you spent this time with the Lord.

DAY 1: WHOEVER . . .

It's often hard to believe in heaven's "whoever" policy when we live in a culture that says you have to be somebody. Status, wealth, class, accomplishments—these matter according to the world's "somebody" policy. They don't according to God's! One on hand, this is good news. We don't have to earn God's love, earn our way to heaven, or earn his grace. On the other hand, it can be hard to let go of our condition that we have to be somebody. We are proud of our accomplishments, wealth, status. We don't always want to discount these things. Read the following verses about heaven's "whoever" policy and then answer the questions below.

Matthew 10:32: *Whoever acknowledges me before men, I will also acknowledge him before my Father in heaven.*

Mark 16:16: *Whoever believes and is baptized will be saved, but whoever does not believe will be condemned.*

John 4:14: *Whoever drinks the water I give him will never thirst.*

John 11:26: *Whoever lives by believing in me will never die.*

Revelation 22:17: *Let the one who is thirsty come; and let the one who wishes take the free gift of the water of life.*

According to your culture, family, or context, what makes a person valuable? Why?

every person is valuable

What gifts does Jesus offer in these verses?

life, salvation, never thirst, not die

What qualifications must you have to receive these gifts? What must you do to be worthy of them?

just believe in Jesus Christ.

What holds you back from believing you are included in heaven's "whoever" policy?

Yes, I am included.

What tends to hold you back from believing that others are included in this policy?

their sins or beliefs.

Prayer: *Father, thank you for including all of us in your "whoever" policy. This is the free gift of grace. This is freedom. While the gifts you offer are good, I can have a hard time accepting them. I am so accustomed to earning my keep that I tend to try and "earn" your love and your grace. Free me from this desire. I also confess that I sometimes think I am more deserving of your gifts than others. Free me from this mindset. Remind me that if I am included as a "whoever," so is my neighbor. Help me to love my neighbors in the way that you love them.*

DAY 2: WHAT DO YOU BELIEVE?

Another key word in this portion of John 3:16 is _believe_: "whoever _believes_ in me will not perish." Perhaps belief comes easily to you. You find it easy to trust in others and take them at their word. Or perhaps it's hard for you to fully believe in _anything_. Read the following story about a doubting believer in the Gospel of Mark and answer the questions below.

> **Mark 9:17–27:** *17 A man in the crowd answered, "Teacher, I brought you my son, who is possessed by a spirit that has robbed him of speech. 18 Whenever it seizes him, it throws him to the ground. He foams at the mouth, gnashes his teeth and becomes rigid. I asked your disciples to drive out the spirit, but they could not."*
>
> *19 "You unbelieving generation," Jesus replied, "how long shall I stay with you? How long shall I put up with you? Bring the boy to me."*
>
> *20 So they brought him. When the spirit saw Jesus, it immediately threw the boy into a convulsion. He fell to the ground and rolled around, foaming at the mouth.*
>
> *21 Jesus asked the boy's father, "How long has he been like this?"*
>
> *"From childhood," he answered. 22 "It has often thrown him into fire or water to kill him. But if you can do anything, take pity on us and help us."*
>
> *23 "'If you can'?" said Jesus. "Everything is possible for one who believes."*
>
> *24 Immediately the boy's father exclaimed, "I do believe; help me overcome my unbelief!"*

25 When Jesus saw that a crowd was running to the scene, he rebuked the impure spirit. "You deaf and mute spirit," he said, "I command you, come out of him and never enter him again."

26 The spirit shrieked, convulsed him violently and came out. The boy looked so much like a corpse that many said, "He's dead." 27 But Jesus took him by the hand and lifted him to his feet, and he stood up.

What is something you believe in without a doubt?

the healing power of Jesus

Why do you think the man came to Jesus to heal his son even when he was unsure of his belief?

He wanted to believe the Jesus could save him.

What does Jesus do as a result of the father's statement in Mark 9:24? What does this tell you about Jesus and how we feel about our belief?

He heals the boy because his father believed.

What is something that would cause you to tell Jesus, "I do believe; help me overcome my unbelief!"? Perhaps it's something theological that you doubt about Jesus, perhaps it's something that you doubt he will do in your life.

the current world and how far from Jesus it is.

Prayer: *Lord, I confess that sometimes I struggle with doubts. I want to believe in my heart that what you say is true but my mind comes up with all kinds of reasons and arguments for why what you say can't be true. Today, I confess along with the father in this story, "I do believe; help me overcome my unbelief!" Instead of hiding my doubts, I will express them to you honestly and allow myself to feel your love—even in the midst of any uncertainties that I have.* Amen

DAY 3: WHAT IS THE TRUTH?

Whoever believes will not perish, but *what* you believe matters. Jesus made this clear to his followers, as did the apostle Paul and others who spread his word after him. It's a tough message for our times but one worth wrestling through, considering how prominent it is in Scripture. What is truth? Can there be many truths? Can you have your *own* truth? Read the following passages that address this question about truth and answer the questions below.

Acts 4:11–12: *11 "For Jesus is the one referred to in the Scriptures, where it says,*

'The stone that you builders rejected
has now become the cornerstone.'

¹² There is salvation in no one else! God has given no
other name under heaven by which we must be saved." (NLT)

1 Corinthians 8:5–6: ⁵ There may be so-called gods both in
heaven and on earth, and some people actually worship many
gods and many lords. ⁶ But for us,

There is one God, the Father,
by whom all things were created,
and for whom we live.
And there is one Lord, Jesus Christ,
through whom all things were created,
and through whom we live. (NLT)

What do you think about truth and salvation? Do you believe
there is one truth or many truths that will get you to the
same destination? Are you unsure? Explain.

*There is only 1 truth about
salvation! It is through
Jesus Christ.*

In Acts 4:11, Jesus is described as a cornerstone. How is Jesus
a cornerstone for our faith?

He is the foundation

In 1 Corinthians 8:5, Paul says that people worship many gods and many lords. What are some gods and lords worshiped in your culture aside from Jesus?

$, things, music, people

Jesus is portrayed as an <u>inclusive Savior</u> (heaven's "whoever" policy) but also exclusive in that he says he is the only way. What do you think about that? Can Jesus be both? Explain your answer.

Anyone is invited to Jesus, but Jesus is the only way.

Prayer: *God, in a world where truth is hard to find and hard to trust, you offer one that I can: whoever believes in Jesus will not perish. Thank you for this truth. Help me cling to it when my belief is weak. Remind me of it when I am tempted to worship other gods and other lords. Teach Jesus' way of grace and truth to me. So often, I either offer one or the other to the people around me. Or I accept one or the other for myself. But Jesus is both. I am so grateful for that. Help me accept his grace and truth in a way that will transform me and how I treat those around me.*

Day 4: A Love That Will Not Let You Go

Perhaps the best part about Jesus' promise in John 3:16 is its · permanence. We cannot lose the promise of salvation once we believe. This is because when we trust in Christ, our very DNA changes. We become God's children—and when you are someone's child, that fact never changes, no matter how distant you become from them or how much times passes between seeing them. Read the following passages about the certainty we can have in our salvation due to our identity through Christ and then answer the questions below.

John 1:11–13: *[11] [Jesus] came to his own, and his own people did not receive him. [12] But to all who did receive him, who believed in his name, he gave the right to become children of God, [13] who were born, not of blood nor of the will of the flesh nor of the will of man, but of God. (ESV)*

Romans 8:14–17: *[14] For those who are led by the Spirit of God are the children of God. [15] The Spirit you received does not make you slaves, so that you live in fear again; rather, the Spirit you received brought about your adoption to sonship. And by him we cry, "Abba, Father." [16] The Spirit himself testifies with our spirit that we are God's children. [17] Now if we are children, then we are heirs—heirs of God and co-heirs with Christ, if indeed we share in his sufferings in order that we may also share in his glory.*

Ephesians 1:13–14: *[13] And you also were included in Christ when you heard the message of truth, the gospel of your salvation. When you believed, you were marked in him with a seal, the promised Holy Spirit,* [14] *who is a deposit guaranteeing our __inheritance__ until the redemption of those who are God's possession—to the praise of his glory.*

Is there an aspect of your "identity" about which you're unsure? (This could be that you're the child of your parents, the husband or wife of your spouse, your ethnicity, race, religion, or even job title.) What causes your uncertainty about this identity?

devil can ~~at try~~ to put ~~doubts~~ in our head. ~~sound~~ They are not true!

Underline or list all the words and phrases in the above passages that suggest family. For example: *child, adoption, heir.* What do these words tell you about your identity to God through Christ?

We are God's family children of God.

According to Romans 8:4–17 and Ephesians 1:13–14, what role does the Holy Spirit play in our adoption by God? Why is this significant?

The Holy Spirit we receive makes us God's children.

Do you feel like you are God's child? Why or why not?

> *Yes — He renews my spirit every morning through His word.*

Prayer: *Father, thank you that I can call you that—Father. When I feel like I don't belong on this earth, I know I belong in your family. When I feel like nothing is certain in my life, I know my identity in Christ as your child cannot change. These are invaluable promises for me. When I grow uncertain of your love for me, or when I begin to doubt my salvation, remind me of this identity. May it root me in your love and assure me of your presence, which is always near.*

FOR NEXT WEEK

Use the space below to write any key points or questions you want to bring to the next group meeting. In preparation for next week, read chapters 10–12 in *3:16*.

THE LAST WORD ON LIFE

"Shall not perish but have eternal life"
John 3:16

WELCOME

What comes to mind when you think about heaven? Puffy clouds, cherubs, and harps? What comes to mind when you think about hell? Fire, brimstone, and horned demons?

Movies, books, and art have all attempted to capture the afterlife—both the good and the bad. We humans, in our finite knowledge and imaginations, want to know what these places will be like, if they exist, and how we end up there. While a plethora of Scripture offers us guidance on these questions, we often jump to so many conclusions of our own that it can be difficult to separate fact from fiction. Because of this, we automatically conjure images of what heaven and hell are like, what we will be like in them, and who else will be there.

Inevitably, our imaginations fail us. They cannot fathom the majesty of heaven, just as they cannot fathom the bitterness of hell. With these otherworldly worlds, we can let our imaginations run wild, but we will always fall short of reality. So, in this final session, we will dig into what Jesus had to say about these places—heaven and hell.

If you've been a Christian for a while, you will likely have some baggage around both words. Perhaps someone used the fear of hell to shame you into belief. Perhaps heaven was reduced to the place your dog or goldfish went. If so, use this time to explore what being in God's presence will be like. Consider the harshness with which Jesus talks about hell as well as the profound promise of an eternity with God. Ask difficult questions. Face your demons, so to speak. Don't shy away from the words that can scare, confuse, and upset you. Instead, see this as safe place to put it all on the table and walk away with the clarity, comfort, and hope that Jesus offers.

SHARE

Begin your time by inviting those in the group to share any insights they had from last week's personal study. Then, to get things started, discuss one of the following questions:

- Name a word or phrase that comes to mind when you think about having a conversation about hell. Why did this come to mind? anguish

— *or* —

- Name a word or phrase that comes to mind when you think about having a conversation about heaven. Why did this come to mind? *love, peace*

READ

Invite someone to read aloud the following passage. Listen for fresh insights as you hear the verse being read and then discuss the questions that follow.

> *⁸ "Then he said to his servants, 'The wedding banquet is ready, but those I invited did not deserve to come. ⁹ So go to the street corners and invite to the banquet anyone you find.' ¹⁰ So the servants went out into the streets and gathered all the people they could find, the bad as well as the good, and the wedding hall was filled with guests.*
>
> *¹¹ "But when the king came in to see the guests, he noticed a man there who was not wearing wedding clothes. ¹² He asked, 'How did you get in here without wedding clothes, friend?' The man was speechless.*
>
> *¹³ "Then the king told the attendants, 'Tie him hand and foot, and throw him outside, into the darkness, where there will be weeping and gnashing of teeth.'*
>
> *¹⁴ "For many are invited, but few are chosen."*
>
> Matthew 22:8–14

What was one key insight that stood out to you from the Scripture? *all are welcome*

What do you think the wedding clothes represent in verse 11?

?

WATCH

Play the video segment for session five (see the streaming video access provided on the inside front cover). As you watch, use the following outline to record any thoughts or concepts that stand out to you.

NOTES

Jesus spoke of hell often. <u>Thirteen percent of his teachings refer to eternal judgment and hell.</u> <u>Two-thirds of his parables relate to resurrection and judgment.</u> Jesus wasn't cruel or capricious, but he was blunt. — *truth*

Hell — everlasting destruction.

Make no mistake: hell is a real place. Words such as *body*, *finger*, and *tongue* presuppose a physical state in which a throat longs for water and a person begs for relief. <u>Hell is an *actual* place populated by physical beings.</u>

hard-hearted who refused God's grace.

God, who is eternally gracious, will never force his will upon anyone. So, in the end, the answer to the puzzling question of how a loving God could send sinners to hell . . . is that he doesn't. They *volunteer*.

Heaven is tangible and touchable. It is as real as the soil in your garden and as physical as the fruit in your orchard. God has already given us glimpses of this future state. These are appetizers of heaven.

You will have assignments in heaven! Just like Adam and Eve in the Garden of Eden, you will have meaningful work to accomplish in your eternal home.

We can believe in the promise that Jesus can replace death with life *because he has already done it.* He has already been down that path and come out the other side. Fully alive. Fully glorified.

DISCUSS

Take some time with your group to discuss what you just
watched and answer the following questions.

1. When was the first time you learned about heaven and
   hell? Who or what (a book or movie, for example) taught
   you about it? How has this education affected the way you
   believe in heaven and hell today?

   Little, in church. Reading books and Bible Studies - learning more.

2. Read Luke 16:19–31. Why did the rich man go to hell?
   How is hell described in this passage?

   He didn't believe.

3. How do you respond to the statement that "hell is reserved
   not for those souls who seek God yet struggle but for those
   who defy God and rebel"? Do you agree or disagree?

   Yes –

4. What is something new that you learned about heaven
   during this session?

   Full of beauty the I/we love.

5. How have your views of heaven and hell affected your view of God and his love for you? Has today's study changed your view of God in any way? If so, how?

God invites all – It's a matter of accepting his invitation. Gives us many chances.

RESPOND

Briefly review the outline for the video teaching and any notes you took. In the space below, write down the most significant point you took away from this session.

PRAY

As you close your time together this week, thank God for this time that you've spent together as a group to study his Word. Thank him for the promise of John 3:16 and the hope of eternal life. Admit if the idea of heaven and hell sometimes feels out of your grasp and ask for a deeper understanding of these topics as you grapple with them. Finally, pray that the truths you know in your heart—that Jesus lived, that Jesus died, and that Jesus was raised and lives again—will be your foundation on which to stand even when you understand everything else. Use the space below to write down any final prayer requests or praises for the coming week.

NAME	REQUEST / PRAISE

FINAL PERSONAL STUDY

SESSION FIVE

Reflect on the material you've covered this week by engaging in any or all of the following activities. Each personal study consists of a passage of Scripture and reflection questions to help you dig deeper into this week's session. The time you invest will be well spent, so let God use it to draw you closer to him. In the coming days, share any key points or insights with one or two of the other group members.

DAY 1: OUR WILL, GOD'S WILL

While hell is already a difficult topic to discuss, what's even more difficult to consider is what was discussed in this week's session: *God doesn't send people to hell*. People choose to go there. We have free will. Our God is not a puppet God. If we reject God, that is *our* choice. It can be difficult to take responsibility for our choices and live with them. It's easier to blame circumstances, others, or even God on what we decide to do. But whether it's eternity, a career move, or a relationship change, we have been given the ability to make our own decisions in our lives. Read what the Bible says about God's will and then answer the questions below.

> **Romans 12:2:** *Do not conform to the pattern of this world, but be transformed by the renewing of your mind. Then you will be able to test and approve what God's will is—his good, pleasing and perfect will.*

> **Ephesians 5:15–20:** *[15] Be very careful, then, how you live—not as unwise but as wise, [16] making the most of every opportunity, because the days are evil. [17] Therefore do not be foolish, but understand what the Lord's will is. [18] Do not get drunk on wine, which leads to debauchery. Instead, be filled with the Spirit, [19] speaking to one another with psalms, hymns, and songs from the Spirit. Sing and make music from your heart to the Lord, [20] always giving thanks to God the Father for everything, in the name of our Lord Jesus Christ.*

> **1 Thessalonians 5:16–18:** *[16] Rejoice always, [17] pray continually, [18] give thanks in all circumstances; for this is God's will for you in Christ Jesus.*

How do you understand God's will, our own free will, and salvation? Where did this understanding coming from?

From teachings and reading the Bible.

According to these verses, what is God's will for our lives?

Live in the spirit
rejoice, give thanks, pray, sing.

How do you reconcile God's will for you but also his giving you freedom of choice? How does this play out in your life?

we have free will to accept or
reject God.

What do you believe is God's will for your life here on earth and in eternity? Why do you believe this?

To be a blessing to others, so
they can see God's love for them.
Save them through God's love.

Prayer: *God, your will is perfect. You want good things for me. I know this in my head—but help me believe this in my heart. I can get confused about what I want for my life and what you want. I can grow fearful that I am making the wrong choices and decisions. I can also neglect my responsibility for those decisions. Show me your way and light my path. Reveal your will to me in your Word and help me make decisions based on the truths that I find there. Thank you for your presence on this path.*

DAY 2: HEAVEN ON EARTH

We often talk about heaven and hell in the ethereal. They are worlds out there, somewhere above or somewhere below.

But when Jesus talked about the kingdom of God, he talked about it as is if he was bringing it now. We miss an opportunity when we only look to eternity for things to be made right and for justice to be done. As Christ followers, we are to continue the work of bringing God's good kingdom to earth. Read what Jesus said about God's kingdom and answer the questions below:

Matthew 6:9–10: *⁹ "This, then, is how you should pray:*

> *"'Our Father in heaven,*
> *hallowed be your name,*
> *¹⁰ your kingdom come,*
> *your will be done,*
> *on earth as it is in heaven.'"*

Mark 1:14–15: *¹⁴ After John was put in prison, Jesus went into Galilee, proclaiming the good news of God. ¹⁵ "The time has come," he said. "The kingdom of God has come near. Repent and believe the good news!"*

Luke 17:20–21: *²⁰ Once, on being asked by the Pharisees when the kingdom of God would come, Jesus replied, "The coming of the kingdom of God is not something that can be observed, ²¹ nor will people say, 'Here it is,' or 'There it is,' because the kingdom of God is in your midst."*

Romans 14:17: *For the kingdom of God is not a matter of eating and drinking, but of righteousness, peace and joy in the Holy Spirit.*

In your own words, what is the kingdom of God to you?

to bring heaven to earth.
to be Christ here on earth, now.

How did Jesus describe and define the kingdom of God in these passages? What point do you think Jesus was trying to get across? Kingdom of God — is what God wants. The kingdom is now — around you.

How did Paul define the kingdom of God in Romans 14:17? What do you think of this definition?

He defined it as righteousness, peace and joy in the holy Spirit.

How could you bring the kingdom of God to earth in your own family, community, or city?

By living like Jesus. Be a light to others. Love others.

Prayer: *"Our Father in heaven, hallowed be your name, your kingdom come, your will be done, on earth as it is in heaven. Give us today our daily bread. And forgive us our debts, as we also have forgiven our debtors. And lead us not into temptation, but deliver us from the evil one" (Matthew 6:9–13).*

DAY 3: HEAVEN IN ETERNITY

The great hope of John 3:16 is that we will not perish but have everlasting life. This is an incredible promise! When the kingdom of God is hard to find on earth, we know it exists because someday we will live there with God and with Jesus. Do you believe that you will be there one day? The assuredness of your own salvation may fluctuate, but it doesn't for God. He has called you. You belong to him. Read the following passages about how you can be certain of your salvation and then answer the questions below.

John 5:24–27: *[24] "Very truly I tell you, whoever hears my word and believes him who sent me has eternal life and will not be judged but has crossed over from death to life. [25] Very truly I tell you, a time is coming and has now come when the dead will hear the voice of the Son of God and those who hear will live. [26] For as the Father has life in himself, so he has granted the Son also to have life in himself. [27] And he has given him authority to judge because he is the Son of Man.*

Romans 10:9–10: *[9] If you declare with your mouth, "Jesus is Lord," and believe in your heart that God raised him from the dead, you will be saved. [10] For it is with your heart that you believe and are justified, and it is with your mouth that you profess your faith and are saved.*

Ephesians 2:6–9: *[6] And God raised us up with Christ and seated us with him in the heavenly realms in Christ Jesus, [7] in*

order that in the coming ages he might show the incompara-
ble riches of his grace, expressed in his kindness to us in Christ
Jesus. ⁸ For it is by grace you have been saved, through faith—
and this is not from yourselves, it is the gift of God—⁹ not by
works, so that no one can boast.

John 3:16: *For God so loved the world that he gave his one*
and only Son, that whoever believes in him shall not perish
but have eternal life.

How did you feel about your salvation at the beginning of
this study as compared to now? Has anything changed? If so,
what and why?

reassurance. Don't doubt.

According to John 5:24–27 and Romans 10:9–10, how are
we saved? Do you feel confident that this is the way we are
saved? Why or why not?

hear my word and believe declare with your mouth.

In Ephesians 2:9, Paul said our salvation is nothing to boast
about. Why does he say this? What does this tell you about
how we are saved?

Because all can be saved. Not saved by works

What, if any, reservations do you have about your own salvation? List them here honestly.

not good enough
didn't do enough

Prayer: *Father, thank you for the assuredness of my salvation. Thank you that it is something that won't go away. Thank you that even when I doubt it, you don't. Fill me with the truth of my own salvation today. Remind me that my identity in you cannot change. Thank you for taking me through this study. Thank you for the people I've been able to learn alongside. Thank you for teaching me more about your Son, my savior Jesus. May I never tire from learning more about him.*

DAY 4: REFLECTIONS

To close out your time in this study, take a few minutes to reflect on what you've learned. You can follow the question prompts below or journal whatever thoughts come to mind.

What did you learn about God?

All are welcome to receive
Christ as their savior.

What did you learn about Jesus?

loving, kind, full of mercy

What did you learn about yourself?

not being honest

What has God revealed to you about eternity, salvation, and the sacrifice of Jesus through the words of John 3:16?

God gave his only Son for us to enter heaven.

Prayer: *Dear God, thank you for this time that I've had in your Word. In just one verse, I have uncovered rich truth. I have grown more confident in your love for me. I have grown more in awe of Jesus' sacrifice for me. Don't let me leave this study unchanged! May these truths transform my heart and mind. May they change the way I think about you, others, and myself. And may they stir me to action in my own community, inspiring me to love others in the way Jesus has loved me. Thank you for the promise of eternal life through your Son. In Jesus' name I pray, amen.*

LEADER'S GUIDE

Thank you for your willingness to lead a group through this study! What you have chosen to do is important, and much good fruit can come from studies like this. The rewards of being a leader are different from those of participating, and we hope that as you lead you will find your own walk with Jesus deepened by this experience of learning about his miracles in the Gospels and what that means for your life today.

3:16 is a five-session Bible study built around video content and small-group interaction. As the group leader, imagine yourself as the host of a dinner party. Your job is to take care of your guests by managing all the behind-the-scenes details so that as your guests arrive, they can focus on each other and on interaction around the topic for that week.

As the group leader, your role is not necessarily to answer all the questions or reteach the content—the video, book, and study guide will do most of that work. Your job is to guide the experience and cultivate your small group into a kind of teaching community. This will make it a place for members to process, question, and reflect—not receive more instruction.

There are several elements in this leader's guide that will help you as you structure your study and reflection time, so follow along and take advantage of each one.

BEFORE YOU BEGIN

Before your first meeting, make sure the group members have a copy of this study guide. Alternately, you can hand out the study guides at your first meeting and give the group members some time to look over the material and ask any preliminary questions. Also make sure they are aware that they have access to the videos at any time through the streaming code provided on the inside front cover. During your first meeting, send a sheet around the room and have the members write down their name, phone number, and email address so you can keep in touch with them during the week.

Generally, the ideal size for a group is between eight to ten people, which ensures everyone will have enough time to participate in discussions. If you have more people, you might want to break up the main group into smaller subgroups. Encourage those who show up at the first meeting to commit to attending the duration of the study, as this will help the group members get to know each other, create stability for the group, and help you know how to prepare each week.

Each of the sessions begins with an opening reflection. The two questions that follow in the "Share" section serve as an icebreaker to get the group members thinking about the topic at hand. You can choose which question you want to ask. Some people may want to tell a long story in response to one of these questions, but the goal is to keep the answers brief. Ideally, you want everyone in the group to get a chance to answer, so try to keep the responses to a minute or less. If you have talkative group members, say up front that everyone needs to limit their answer to one minute.

Give the group members a chance to answer but tell them to feel free to pass if they wish. With the rest of the study, it's generally not a good idea to have everyone answer every question—a free-flowing discussion is more desirable. But with the opening icebreaker questions, you can go around the circle. Encourage shy people to share, but don't force them.

Before your first meeting, let the group members know that each session contains four between-sessions studies. While these are optional, it will help the members cement the concepts presented during the group study time and encourage them to spend time each day in God's Word. Let them know that if they choose to do so, they can watch the video for the following week by accessing the streaming code found on the inside front cover of their studies. Also invite them to bring any questions and insights they uncovered while reading to your next meeting, especially if they had a breakthrough moment or didn't understand something.

WEEKLY PREPARATION

As the leader, there are a few things you should do to prepare for each meeting:

- *Read through the session.* This will help you to become familiar with the content and know how to structure the discussion times.
- *Decide how the videos will be used.* Determine whether you want the members to watch the videos ahead of time (via the streaming access code found on the inside front cover) or together as a group.

- *Decide which questions you definitely want to discuss.* Based on the amount and length of group discussion, you may not be able to get through all of the Bible study and group discussion questions, so choose four to five questions that you definitely want to cover.
- *Be familiar with the questions you want to discuss.* When the group meets, you'll be watching the clock, so you want to make sure you are familiar with the questions you have selected. In this way, you'll ensure you have the material more deeply in your mind than your group members.
- *Pray for your group.* Pray for your group members throughout the week and ask God to lead them as they study his Word.
- *Bring extra supplies to your meeting.* The members should bring their own pens for writing notes, but it's a good idea to have extras available for those who forget. You may also want to bring paper and additional Bibles.

Note that in many cases there will be no one "right" answer to the question. Answers will vary, especially when the group members are being asked to share their personal experiences.

STRUCTURING THE DISCUSSION TIME

You will need to determine with your group how long you want to meet each week so you can plan your time accordingly. Generally, most groups like to meet for either sixty minutes or ninety minutes, so you could use one of the following schedules:

SECTION	60 MINUTES	90 MINUTES
Welcome (members arrive and get settled)	5 minutes	10 minutes
Share (discuss one of the opening questions for the session)	10 minutes	15 minutes
Video (watch the teaching material together and take notes)	15 minutes	15 minutes
Group Discussion and Response (discuss the Bible study questions you selected ahead of time)	25 minutes	40 minutes
Prayer/Closing (pray together as a group and dismiss)	5 minutes	10 minutes

As the group leader, it is up to you to keep track of the time and keep things moving along according to your schedule. You might want to set a timer for each segment so both you and the group members know when your time is up. (Note there are some good phone apps for timers that play a gentle chime or other pleasant sound instead of a disruptive noise.)

Don't be concerned if the group members are quiet or slow to share. People are often quiet when they are pulling together their ideas, and this might be a new experience for them. Just ask a question and let it hang in the air until someone shares. You can then say, "Thank you. What about others?"

GROUP DYNAMICS

Leading a group through *3:16* will prove to be highly reward-ing both to you and your group members. However, this doesn't mean you will not encounter any challenges along the way. Discussions can get off track. Group members may not be sensitive to the needs and ideas of others. Some might worry they will be expected to talk about matters that make them feel awkward. Others may express comments that result in disagreements. To help ease this strain on you and the group, consider the following ground rules:

- When someone raises a question or comment that is off topic, suggest you deal with it another time, or, if you feel led to go in that direction, let the group know you will be spending some time discussing it.
- If someone asks a question you don't know how to answer, admit it and move on. At your discretion, feel free to invite group members to comment on questions that call for personal experience.
- If you find one or two people are dominating the discussion time, direct a few questions to others in the group. Outside the main group time, ask the more dominating members to help you draw out the quieter ones. Work to make them a part of the solution instead of the problem.
- When a disagreement occurs, encourage the group members to process the matter in love. Encourage those on opposite sides to restate what they heard the other side say about the matter, and then invite each

side to evaluate if that perception is accurate. Lead the group in examining other Scriptures related to the topic and look for common ground.

When any of these issues arise, encourage your group members to follow these words from the Bible: "Love one another" (John 13:34), "If it is possible, as far as it depends on you, live at peace with everyone" (Romans 12:18), "Whatever is true . . . noble . . . right . . . if anything is excellent or praiseworthy—think about such things" (Philippians 4:8), and "Be quick to listen, slow to speak and slow to become angry" (James 1:19). This will make your group time more rewarding and beneficial for everyone who attends.

Thank you again for your willingness to lead your group. May God reward your efforts and dedication and make your time together in *3:16* fruitful for his kingdom.

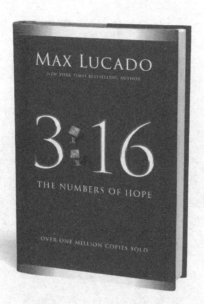

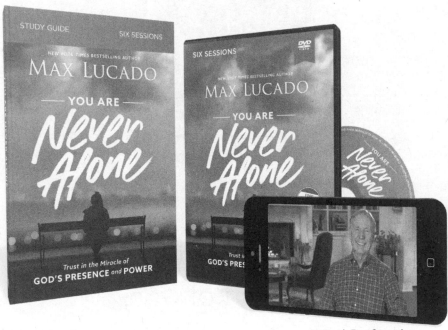

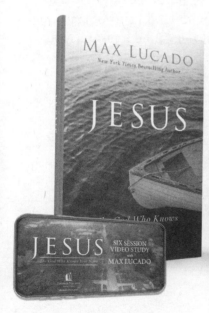
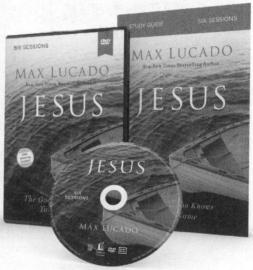

CELEBRATE EASTER, CHRISTMAS, AND THE LIFE AND MINISTRY OF JESUS

In *Because of Bethlehem*, a four-session video Bible study, Max Lucado explores how the One who made everything chose to make himself nothing and come into our world. Jesus' birth gives us the promise that God is always near us, always for us, and always within us—and that we no longer need to have marks on our record.

In *He Chose the Nails*, a five-session video Bible study, Max continues by examining the gifts that Christ gave at his crucifixion. These include not only the gift of the cross but also the gift of the thorns, the nails, and the empty tomb. The cross is rich with God's gifts of grace, and as we unwrap them, we will hear him whisper, "I did it just for you."

| Book | Christmas Study Guide | DVD | Easter Study Guide | Book |
| 9780849947599 | 9780310687054 | 9780310687849 | 9780310687269 | 9780718085070 |

Available now at your favorite bookstore,
or streaming video on StudyGateway.com.

GOD HAS A CURE FOR YOUR WORRIES

Anxiety doesn't have to dominate life. Max looks at seven admonitions from the Apostle Paul in Philippians 4:4–8 that lead to one wonderful promise: "The peace of God which surpasses all understanding." He shows how God is ready to give comfort to help us face the calamities in life, view bad news through the lens of sovereignty, discern the lies of Satan, and tell ourselves the truth. We can discover true peace from God that surpasses all human understanding.

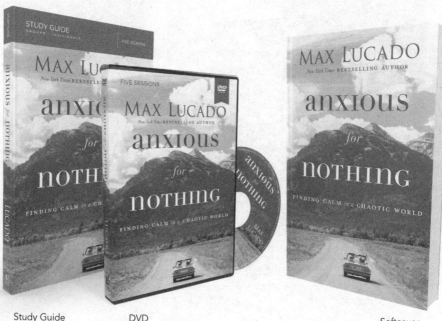

Study Guide
9780310087311

DVD
9780310087335

Softcover
9780718074210

Available now at your favorite bookstore,
or streaming video on StudyGateway.com.

THERE IS A PATH TO HAPPINESS THAT ALWAYS DELIVERS

In this book and video Bible study, Max Lucado shares the unexpected path to a lasting happiness, one that produces reliable joy in any season of life. Based on the teachings of Jesus and backed by modern research, *How Happiness Happens* presents a surprising but practical way of living that will change you from the inside out.

Study Guide
9780310105718

DVD with Free Streaming Access
9780310105732

Book
9780718096137

Available now at your favorite bookstore,
or streaming video on StudyGateway.com.

40 ▶ DAYS THROUGH THE BOOK

Study Books of the Bible
with Trusted Pastors

The 40 Days Through the Book series has been designed to help believers more actively engage with God's Word. Each study encourages participants to read through one book in the New Testament at least once during the course of 40 days and provides them with:

- A clear understanding of the background and culture in which the book was written,
- Insights into key passages of Scripture, and
- Clear applications and takeaways from the particular book that participants can apply to their lives.

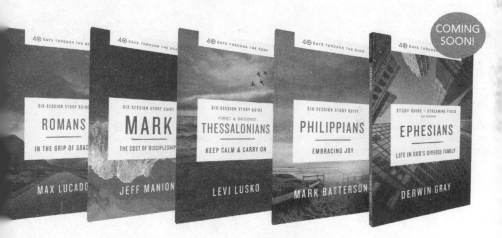

Available now at your favorite bookstore, or streaming video on StudyGateway.com.

HarperChristian Resources